First World War
and Army of Occupation
War Diary
France, Belgium and Germany

57 DIVISION
170 Infantry Brigade
Loyal North Lancashire Regiment
2/5th Battalion (Territorial Force)
8 November 1915 - 29 February 1916

WO95/2979/2

The Naval & Military Press Ltd
www.nmarchive.com
Published in association with The National Archives

Published by

The Naval & Military Press Ltd

Unit 10 Ridgewood Industrial Park,
Uckfield, East Sussex,
TN22 5QE England
Tel: +44 (0) 1825 749494

www.naval-military-press.com
www.nmarchive.com

This diary has been reprinted in facsimile from the original. Any imperfections are inevitably reproduced and the quality may fall short of modern type and cartographic standards.

© Crown Copyright
Images reproduced by permission of The National Archives, London, England, 2015.

Contents

Document type	Place/Title	Date From	Date To
Heading	WO95/2979-2		
Heading	War Diary Of The 2/5th Bn Loyal Nth Lancs Regt For The Month Of September 1915		
War Diary		00/09/1915	00/09/1915
Miscellaneous	170th Infantry Brigade	03/09/1915	03/09/1915
Heading	War Diary Of 2/5 Bn L.N. Lancs Reg From 1 Oct 1915 To 31 Oct 1915 Volume I		
War Diary	Ashford	00/10/1900	00/10/1900
Heading	War Diary Of 2nd Line 5th Bn. Loyal W. Lancs Regt From 1st Novr 1915 To 30th Novr 1915 Volume I		
War Diary	Beachborough	08/11/1915	18/11/1915
War Diary	Ashford	23/11/1915	23/11/1915
War Diary	Bilsington	25/11/1915	25/11/1915
War Diary	Hythe & Dymchurch	27/11/1915	27/11/1915
War Diary	Warren Halt	27/11/1915	27/11/1915
Heading	War Diary Of 2/5th Bn. Loyal W.Lancs Regt. From 1st Decr 1915 To 31st Decr 1915		
War Diary	Ashford	03/12/1915	03/12/1915
War Diary	Bilsington	07/12/1915	07/12/1915
War Diary	Beachborough	20/12/1915	20/12/1915
Heading	War Diary Of 2/5th Bn. Loyal N. Lancs. Regt From 1st January 1916 To 31st January 1916 (Volume 3)		
War Diary	Ashford	01/01/1916	17/01/1916
War Diary	Beachborough	18/01/1916	18/01/1916
War Diary	Ashford	19/01/1916	31/01/1916
Heading	War Diary Of 2/5th Bn. Loyal N. Lancs. Regt From 1st February 1916 To 29th February 1916 (Volume IV)		
War Diary	Ashford	01/02/1916	29/02/1916

WO 95/29779(b)

17e BDE

CONFIDENTIAL.

WAR DIARY.

of the

15th Bn. Loyal No Lanc Regt

for the month of SEPTEMBER, 1915.

Army Form C. 2118.

WAR DIARY
or
INTELLIGENCE SUMMARY

(Erase heading not required.)

Instructions regarding War Diaries and Intelligence Summaries are contained in F. S. Regs., Part II. and the Staff Manual respectively. Title pages will be prepared in manuscript.

Hour, Date, Place	Summary of Events and Information	Remarks and references to Appendices
September, 1915.	NIL.	

[signature]
Lieut Colonel.
Comdg. 2/5th Batt. Loyal North Lancs Regt.

Unit........ 2/5th Bn. Loyal North Lancs Rgt.
Brigade ..... 170th Infantry Brigade
Division.....57th (West Lancs) Division.
Mobilization Centre.......Bolton.
Temporary War Station. Ashford. KENT.

Stations since occupied subsequent to Concentration
Blackpool. Sevenoaks. Oxted.

MOBILIZATION

CONCENTRATION AT WAR STATIONS (including railway moves)

ORGANIZATION FOR DEFENCE.

TRAINING This is being seriously retarded for lack of training areas. Efficient training in outpost duties has been difficult, and in artillery formations almost impossible since May when the Unit was at Sevenoaks, for lack of large enough areas.

The men are also getting rusty in the use of the .303 rifle of which this Unit has been totally deprived. The .256 rifle does not form a satisfactory substitute Efficiency in rapid firing is a matter requiring sufficient practice for for the motions to become automatic and instinctive. Consequently a change of rifle is fatal to efficiency and practice with the one does not qualify for use of the other type of arm.

Under existing regulations none of our last 422 recruits can fire on the open range. We have no .303 rifles and we have already fired our full allowance of .256 ammunition.

DISCIPLINE

ADMINISTRATION

REORGANIZATION OF T.F. INTO HOME AND IMPERIAL SERVICE

PREPARATION OF UNITS FOR IMPERIAL SERVICE

Before this Unit can be made fit for Imperial Service the following points will have to receive attention.

1. Something over 25% of the men are rejected on account of bad teeth, but all remediable.

The rate at which these men can be attended to under existing arrangements is about 36 weekly at which rate it will be at leats two months before the work can be completed.

2. About 20% of the last 422 recruits are medically unfit for Imperial Service. These men will have to be removed to some Home Service Unit and replaced by fresh recruits who in turn will require further training. Unless about 100 recruits are sent for every 80 vacancies, exactly the same progress will have to be gone through again. Every day's delay in relieving this Unit of these unfit men puts back the time when the Unit can be ready for Imperial Service at full strength.

3. Provision will have to be made for the last 422 recruits and for the 100 men or so, who will be required to fill the places of those of them who are medically unfit, to fire the musketry course. See remarks under training.

4. 38 of my paper strength are non effectives being bandsmen on duty with the Administrative Centre.

Ashford
Sept 3/15.

Lieut. Colonel.
Cmdg 2/5th Bn. L.N. Lancs Rgt.

Confidential

War Diary
of
2/5 Bn L. N. Lanc Reg.

From 1 Oct 1915 to 31 Oct 1915.

Volume I

Army Form C. 2118.

WAR DIARY
or
INTELLIGENCE SUMMARY.
(Erase heading not required.)

Place	Date	Hour	Summary of Events and Information	Remarks and references to Appendices
Ashford	October		NIL	

Thomson
Lieut Colonel
Comdg. 95th Bn Loyal North Lancs Regt.

Confidential

War Diary

of

2nd Line 5th Bn. Loyal N. Lancs. Regt.

from 1st Novr. 1915, to 30th Novr. 1915.

Volume
I.

Army Form C. 2118.

WAR DIARY
or
INTELLIGENCE SUMMARY.

(Erase heading not required.)

Place	Date	Hour	Summary of Events and Information	Remarks and references to Appendices
Brackborough	6/11/15		Observation Post. 1 Officer & 74 other ranks established.	B.H.
-do-	15/11/15		Observation Post relieved by 1 Officer and 7 other ranks.	B.H.
Ashford	23/11/15		Inspection of Dallas by Major General E.J. Dickson, Inspector of Infantry.	B.H.
Dissington	25/11/15		Observation Post. 1 Officer & 74 other ranks established	B.H.
Hythe & Dymchurch	27/11/15		Two Officers & 75 other ranks relieved 2/15 Kent Cyclist Bn. in Coast patrol duties.	B.H.
Havren Hall	27/11/15		One Officer & 15 Other ranks relieved 2/1st Kent Cyclist Bn. in Coast patrol duties	B.H.

Thomson
Lieut. Colonel
Comdg. 2nd Line 3rd Bn. Royal N. Lancs. Regt.

Confidential.

War Diary
of
2/5th Bn. Loyal N. Lancs. Regt.

from 1st Decr. 1915, to 31st Decr. 1915.

Army Form C. 2118.

WAR DIARY
or
INTELLIGENCE SUMMARY.
(Erase heading not required.)

Place	Date	Hour	Summary of Events and Information	Remarks and references to Appendices
ASHFORD	3/12/15		Establishment of Officers reduced in accordance with W.O. 2793 A.G.=1.12.15	124.
—"—	3/12/15		Inspection of Officers books by L.O.C. 57th (W.Lanc.) Divn.	124.
BILSINGTON	7/12/15		Observation post (1 Offr. 4 O.R.) relieved by Devon Cyclist Bn.	124.
BEACHBOROUGH	20/12/15		Observation post (1 Offr. 7 O.R.) relieved by party of similar strength	124.

Wunworth
Major
for Lieut. Colonel
Comdg. 2/5 Royal N. Lancs. Regt.
A.O.D.

Confidential.

War Diary

— of —

2/5th Bn. Loyal N. Lancs. Regt.

from 1st January, 1916, to 31st January, 1916.

(Volume 3.)

Army Form C. 2118.

WAR DIARY

INTELLIGENCE SUMMARY.

(Erase heading not required.)

Instructions regarding War Diaries and Intelligence Summaries are contained in F. S. Regs., Part II. and the Staff Manual respectively. Title pages will be prepared in manuscript.

Place	Date	Hour	Summary of Events and Information	Remarks and references to Appendices
ASHFORD	1/1/16	NIL		B.M.
"	2/1/16	NIL		B.M.
"	3/1/16		O.C. Bn. proceeded overseas on instructional tour	B.M.
"	4/1/16	NIL		B.M.
"	5/1/16	NIL		B.M.
"	6/1/16	NIL		B.M.
"	7/1/16		O.C. Bn. rejoined from overseas instructional tour	B.M.
"	8/1/16	NIL		B.M.
"	9/1/16	NIL		B.M.
"	10/1/16		Inspection of messing centres by G.O.C. 57th Divn.	B.M.
"	11/1/16		Inspection of Battn. at work by G.O.C. 2nd Army.	B.M.
"	12/1/16	NIL		B.M.
"	13/1/16	NIL		B.M.
"	14/1/16	NIL		B.M.
"	15/1/16	NIL		B.M.
"	16/1/16	NIL		B.M.

1577 Wt. W10791/1773 500,000 1/15 D. D. & L. A.D.S.S./Forms/C. 2118.

Army Form C. 2118.

WAR DIARY

INTELLIGENCE SUMMARY.

(Erase heading not required.)

Instructions regarding War Diaries and Intelligence Summaries are contained in F. S. Regs., Part II. and the Staff Manual respectively. Title pages will be prepared in manuscript.

Place	Date	Hour	Summary of Events and Information	Remarks and references to Appendices
ASHFORD.	17/1/16		NIL	B.M.
BEACHBOROUGH.	18/1/16		Observation post (1 Off. 7 O.R.) relieved by party of similar strength	B.M.
ASHFORD.	19/1/16		NIL	B.M.
" "	20/1/16		NIL	B.M.
" "	21/1/16		NIL	B.M.
" "	22/1/16		NIL	B.M.
" "	23/1/16		NIL	B.M.
" "	24/1/16		NIL	B.M.
" "	25/1/16		NIL	B.M.
" "	26/1/16		NIL	B.M.
" "	27/1/16		NIL	B.M.
" "	28/1/16		NIL	B.M.
" "	29/1/16		NIL	B.M.
" "	30/1/16		NIL	B.M.
" "	31/1/16		Inspection of Battn. by G.O.C., 170th Infy. Bde.	B.M.

Thomson
Lieut. Colonel,
Comdg. 25th Bn. Royal W. Lancs. Regt.

Confidential.

War Diary
of
2/5th Bn. Loyal N. Lancs. Regt.

from 1st February 1916, to 29th February 1916.

(Volume IV.)

Army Form C. 2118.

WAR DIARY
INTELLIGENCE SUMMARY.
(Erase heading not required.)

Instructions regarding War Diaries and Intelligence Summaries are contained in F. S. Regs., Part II. and the Staff Manual respectively. Title pages will be prepared in manuscript.

Place	Date	Hour	Summary of Events and Information	Remarks and references to Appendices
ASHFORD	1/2/16	NIL		10th.
"	2/2/16	NIL		10th.
"	3/2/16	NIL		24h.
"	4/2/16	NIL		10th.
"	5/2/16	NIL		10th.
"	6/2/16	NIL		13th.
"	7/2/16	NIL		10th.
"	8/2/16	NIL		10th.
"	9/2/16	NIL		10th.
"	10/2/16	NIL		10th.
"	11/2/16	NIL		10th.
"	12/2/16	NIL		10th.
"	13/2/16	NIL		10th.
"	14/2/16	NIL		10th.
"	15/2/16	NIL		10th.
"	16/2/16	NIL		13th.

Army Form C. 2118.

WAR DIARY

INTELLIGENCE SUMMARY

(Erase heading not required.)

Instructions regarding War Diaries and Intelligence Summaries are contained in F.S. Regs., Part II. and the Staff Manual respectively. Title pages will be prepared in manuscript.

Place	Date	Hour	Summary of Events and Information	Remarks and references to Appendices
ASHFORD	17/2/16	NIL		12th
— " —	18/2/16	NIL		12th
— " —	19/2/16	NIL		12th
— " —	20/2/16	NIL		12th
— " —	21/2/16	NIL		12th
— " —	22/2/16	NIL		12th
— " —	23/2/16		Packing trials, transport-vehicles. (57th Divn. Order No. 425, of 19.2.16).	12th
— " —	24/2/16	5.35 P.M.	Batn. as unit of 170th Infy. Bde. held in readiness to move	12th
— " —	25/2/16		— do —	12th
— " —	26/2/16		— do —	12th
— " —	27/2/16		— do —	12th
— " —	28/2/16		— do — Inspection of books by G.O.C. 170th Infy. Bde.	12th
— " —	29/2/16		— do —	12th

T. Thomason
Lieut. Colonel
Comdg. 2/5th Bn. Royal N. Lancs. Regt.

www.ingramcontent.com/pod-product-compliance
Lightning Source LLC
Chambersburg PA
CBHW081510160426
43193CB00014B/2641